Embraced by Love

Poems by Tanis Helliwell

Copyright © Tanis Helliwell 2008

All rights reserved. Reproduction or utilization of this work in any form, by any means now known or hereinafter invented, including, but not limited to, xerography, photocopying and recording, and in any known storage and retrieval system, is forbidden without permission from the copyright holder.

Cover design by Janet Rouss
Cover photograph by Tanis Helliwell
Interior design Robert Dufour and Blitzprint

Library and Archives Canada Cataloguing in Publication

Helliwell, Tanis,
    Embraced by love : poems / by Tanis Helliwell.

ISBN 978-0-9809033-1-7

1. Love poetry, Canadian (English). 2. Spiritual life--Poetry. I. Title.
PS8615.E437E43 2008   C811'.6 C2008-900188-5

Published by The International Institute for Transformation
www.iitransform.com

Printed and bound in Canada

Dedication

This book is dedicated to all lovers. To you who commit your lives to keeping your hearts open to your beloved, your family and friends, to spirit, and to the world.

Poetry

True poetry flows from one's core
distilled, pure, honest.
Like an arrow it hits its victim
right in the heart,
dealing a death blow to deceit and falsehood
prying open the armour and letting in Light.

Table of Contents

                                                Pages

Introduction
- Love — 11

Part I: Embraced by Eros — 19

- Embracing the Green Man — 21
- Dining on Love, Celebrating Lovers — 22
- Unwrapping the Gift — 23
- Womanhood Reclaimed — 24
- Four of Us — 25
- Stage Two: Disenchantment — 26
- Two Kinds of Food — 27
- A Wasted Heart, More or Less? — 28
- Pain, Similarities and Differences — 29
- No Illusions — 30
- Valour — 31
- Stage Three: Non-Attachment — 32
- Between Two Knowns — 33
- Three Possibilities — 34
- The Truth — 35
- Ups and Downs — 36
- Stage Four: Companionship — 37
- Gratitude — 38
- Between the Sheets, Chatty Kathy — 39
- A Gentle Man — 40
- In Love and Love — 41

Part II: Embraced by Philia   43

We Never Loved Like This Before	45
Two Men	46
Dream Lovers	47
Dark Thanksgiving	48
As Mortality Hovers	49
Mammisi	50
To Mother, Grieving Your Absence	51
Lucie	52
Sammy	54
To Wayshowers	55
Ode to Nutcrackers	56
A Good Teacher	57

Part III: Embraced by Agape   59

Gold Filings	61
Comrades on the Path	62
Dress Up, The Mirror	63
Hold Your Note	64
Feast on Me, Rebirth	65
Awakening from Success	66
September Melancholy	67
Choices	68
Enjoy the Day	69
Loving the World	70
A Prayer for God's Grace	71
Salute to Death	72

Insight	73
Day of Liberation, The Beloved	74
Allow	75
Message for Doubting Thomas	76
Cease Talking and Listen	77
Playing with Matter	78
Rainbow Dust	79
Do You Want This?	80
The Last Word	81

Quatrains   **83**

Part IV: Embraced by Nature   **91**

Wake Up	93
Amaryllis, Birth of the Day	94
Two Days at Best, Ode to Rhubarb	95
Bravery or Trust	96
Birds I Loved Today	97
Winter Feeding	98
Abundance	99
The Eagle Doesn't Give Up, Always Another Fish	100
The Nervous Doe	101
When Civilization Meets Nature	102

About the Author   **104**

Other Books, CDs, DVDs   **105**

Acknowledgments

The poems in *Embraced by Eros* would never have been birthed if not for my dear friend WB. Thank you for the many gifts of love that you have given me and for generously sharing our journey with others.

Much of the poetry in *Embraced by Love* has as its underpinning a love of the divine. For more than twenty years I have taught the mystical spiritual traditions of the world, but I have not shared my poetry, as it is deeply personal and I am, by nature, private. This year I took the plunge and read my poems to students in the International Institute for Transformation who encouraged me to offer them to others. For this and the many ways they have taught me agape love, I give thanks.

I also wish to thank Barbara Siskind, Ann Mortifee, Jill McBeath, John Donlan and Monika Bernegg, my German translator for editorial suggestions. Thanks also to readers Connie Phenix, Willa Miniely, Jenny Linley, Marielle Croft, Simon Llewellyn and to Janet Rouss who produced the beautiful cover.

Love

Love is arguably the most important feeling that we can experience in our lives. It motivates us to be the best of what we are capable of being, and the worst. More books, films and songs are devoted to the exploration of love than to any other topic. We know that babies who are held and cuddled thrive, and that babies deprived of touch wither and even die. As adults the quest to be in loving relationships continues and without it we feel sad and depressed.

There are many kinds of love, but the three main ones defined by the ancient Greeks are *Eros, Philia*, and *Agape*. It is helpful to examine these terms in order to better understand how love affects our lives.

Eros

Eros is love of the physical body. It is the sexual attraction that we feel for one person instead of another. It fires up our gonads and juices and creates a hunger, a lust, in our physical bodies. Eros is also sensual and can be found in the bodily pleasures of enjoying a massage, having our feet scratched, or our head stroked. The many forms of grooming, manicures, pedicures, and even having our hair cut are sensual outlets for eros in our society, and sometimes the only forms available to us when we do not have a lover.

Eros overturns emotional stability with passion and dominates our thoughts with those of the object of our desire. It can wreak havoc in our lives when we leave stable relationships and jobs to follow the new person whom we think we love. This stage of erotic love might only last from three to six months, but oh what a ride. During this time we project on our lover all the desirable qualities that we'd like him or her to have, and carefully avoid examining any attributes that lie outside our fantasy.

Eros comes in many degrees from mild infatuation to passionate intensity where we feel that we might die if our beloved does not reciprocate our love. Yet, in time the erotic charge between lovers diminishes, and we wake up and see the previously ignored qualities of our lover and start to re-assess our relationship. Questions arise about our lover's values, lifestyle, friends, and we examine these to see if they fit with ours. If do not, the relationship will most often end, although sometimes the erotic component remains strong and individuals stay in relationships that are not healthy in other ways. If, however, we end up liking our lover as a friend then we enter the second stage of love, which in Greek is called *philia*.

Philia

Philia is the love we have for our family members and good friends. It is affectionate and platonic. It is love of the heart, not love of the gonads. When we think of the love we have for our mother, sister, brother, and both men and women friends we understand philia. This love transcends gender, age, and is a love of someone who is part of our circle, someone whom we love as a person, who feels known to us and with whom we share our personal lives. This love might also include a love of a dog, cat, or bird who is part of our family.

Arranged marriages in eastern countries very often start with philia love where spouses are chosen by the parents from families who share similar values and friendship. Most often the children have had neither sexual experience, nor erotic feelings for their spouse at the time of marriage, but over time erotic love may blossom from philia. Love in western countries is the opposite where individuals most often fall in love with eros and through time develop philia love. Interestingly, spouses in eastern countries appear to have as much success with loving marriages by starting relationships based on philia, as western countries do by starting relationships based on eros. It appears that philia is important for long-term loving relationships.

Agape

There is a third kind of love. Agape is the love that God, The Creator, The Beloved, The Great Mother, and Spirit by all names, has for us and for all life. Agape is used in the New Testament of the Bible to describe the unconditional way in which God loves us and that we can emulate by loving others. It is defined by the Buddhist expression "Love all beings as you love your mother," or as Jesus said, "Love thy neighbour as thyself." At first glance these expressions might be confusing, as we have just said that philia is the term given to love of family members. However, with a deeper look we can see that both Buddha and Jesus are emphasising unconditional love for all beings.

Agape love has neither the hot passion of eros, nor the conditional exclusivity and familiarity of philia. It is a more spiritual love than the other two, and has at its foundation the belief that all beings are one. When we love with agape, we do not kill others from a different country, religion, or way of life than ours. We hold all life as sacred and as an expression of spirit in its many forms. We may not like what someone is doing, but we still love him or her. Unlike philia and eros's preferences and selectivity, agape has no preferences about whom or what it loves. Agape is altruistic, wide open and not sentimental.

Agape is also known as the love of the soul and it is the love of a spiritual seeker, who loves God and does whatever it takes, be it dark nights or bliss, to unite with the divine. Agape is non-attached to results, and is committed to being love, fully in the present moment with whomever, and whatever, is occurring.

Eros, philia and agape are not mutually exclusive and we can love a person, and even the divine, with all three kinds of love. In our world we have a better understanding and experience of both eros and philia than we do of agape. Because agape is cooler and non-attached, it may not always be recognized as love. Teachers who help us on our spiritual path practice agape. They might use both compassion and tough love with their students, in order to teach them agape, which are to love all beings as they love a beloved, a mother, or spirit.

All three forms of love motivate us to become better people. Through erotic love we experience the heights of ecstasy, and the depths of yearning and pain so that our hearts are cracked open to love more. Through philia love we learn forgiveness, patience, tolerance and endurance in committing to love another individual long-term. Through agape we develop unlimited compassion, faith and trust for all the ways in which spirit works through love in our world.

Nature

Arguably, there are even more kinds of love than eros, philia, and agape including love of music, philosophy and various cultures. Poetry is highly personal and individual and this collection *Embraced by Love* is a reflection of the various ways in which I love and have loved. Therefore, I include one other form of love, which is that of nature.

Nature is a reflection of the divine, and loving animals, birds, trees, and all beings of the Earth is another way of loving spirit. My personal journey has been one of deepening commitment to spirit and to the love that creates and sustains all life. As a child, this love was of nature and the bliss I experienced in sunrises, sunsets, falling rain and scent of flowers. Even as an adult I continue to encounter the divine in nature, and the older I become the more my life aligns to the heartbeat of the Earth and the natural world. I was unable to express these feelings as a child and, thankfully while young, I discovered William Wordsworth and other nature poets, as they were able to express in words what I could only feel.

Poetry, in fact, has shed light on my journey of love throughout my life. In my late teens, I underwent a near death experience, which catapulted me into a deeper longing to commune with spirit. I was introduced, soon afterwards, to T. S. Eliot's *Four*

Quartets, and found that he moved through the depths and heights of longing for God that I had.

When in my thirties I went through a dark night of the soul, once again I turned to poetry to help me uncover and express my spiritual feelings of isolation. This time it was the German poet Rilke and his *Duino Elegies* that befriended me.

In recent years, the path to God has taken other forms. Dark humour, emotional twists, experiencing simultaneously both the pleasure and pain of life, have become my companions and underlying these I have an ever-deepening trust and faith in spirit. The classic Persian poets Rumi and Hafiz, the Chinese Chang Tzu, and the Indian Kabir have accompanied me on this journey as I have rediscovered the divine in each person and in the world-perfect-just as it is. And as my womanhood blossoms again, I find that the contemporary women poets, Mary Oliver and Jane Hirshfield with their down to earth sensual spirituality, touch me.

The poetry that speaks to me–both my own and that of others–evokes the mystery of spirit in its beautiful forms–be it lovers, friends, nature, or God. A term sometimes used to describe this kind of poetry is 'sacred poetry' because it contains teaching lessons that assist us in our spiritual transformation. Many of the poems in *Embraced by Love* are written with this intention.

I wish to share with you some of the places where love has taken me. Although I have divided the collection into four sections, *Eros, Philia, Agape* and *Nature*, some poems thematically could be placed in more than one category. For example, for ease of reading, I have kept all poems to do with the many stages of love experienced with a lover in the category *Eros*. Also, I have included poems to spiritual teachers and companions under *Philia*, because of the feeling of friendship that I feel towards them. The poems, which describe my love of God and learning on my spiritual journey, are found in the section *Agape*.

I embrace you and welcome you into my deepest heart. I hope these poems will shed light on your path, express the feelings in your heart, and give you joy and peace.

Tanis Helliwell

Embraced by Eros

When you have fasted and prayed,
prodded and probed your depths,
burnt candles and done rituals,
analyzed your belly button to death,
you can go no further.

Then, only a lover can help.

Embracing the Green Man

If you love nature
fertile and vibrant,
living things–all manner of them
precious to you,
how can you not love the Green Man,
deep sadness in ocean eyes.

How can you not revel
awakened from deep sleep of winter
when spring gushes forth
in your body transformed.

Celebrating Lovers

How did I arrive
in this verdant land,
wet and sweet and lazy?

I was a desert dweller
wrapped up tight against the wind,
dry and cautious
sipping one drop a day.

Dining on Love

Only an empty husk
   bled of desire,
   restrained from eating,
   co-operative in God's will,
could come to love's table
wondering what to do.

Unwrapping the Gift

Enticed by signs
too strong for chance,
I entered the unknown
into your arms.

"How beautiful," you exclaimed
opening the gift,
and the wrapping paper fell away
leaving me naked.

How little it took:
a few kind words and your apples,
for eons of independence to crumble
wanting again to be loved.

Womanhood Reclaimed

Love in middle-age,
juices flowing suddenly
again.
Caught me by surprise
being fifteen a second time,
shy, nervous and yearning.

Still....
how nice to be alone
after nights of passion,
exhausted, relaxed, full of you,
enjoying my space
that is yours
sometimes.

Four of Us

Two of you sitting there:
the eager lover wanting release from pain,
escape in pleasure.

The other-the old sage holding aloof,
untouched and cool,
knowing, as sure as the sun rises,
tomorrow will look after itself.

Two of me sitting here:
the young virgin, her first time
bleeding when entered,
heart opening in innocent trust.

The other-an old wise woman,
sensible from suffering,
urging retreat.

Stage Two: Disenchantment

The rainbow dissolves
revealing dark clouds,
geese gather to fly south,
dew lies heavy on the ground.

Melancholy holds my heart
as I balance yearning and 'what is.'
Truth is an unrelenting teacher.

You say, "All is illusion"
but this does not help,
cold words mouthed without passion.

Living in my skin now
is a thirsty woman
wanting love-giving and receiving,
filling her until, like a car, she's all tanked up.

Two Kinds of Food

Lifted off my feet
I was taken to a foreign land
where, shown beauty, tasting ambrosia,
my heart cracked open.

Overcome with passion, I spoke of love
and you gently closed the door,
bringing me back to reality
to eat organic food.

Ah...there are subtle channels
unknown to science longing to be filled,
only opened by eyes of love,
and whispered endearments.

This food I also crave.

A Wasted Heart

Reflect on those who die of wasting.
Ah, you think I speak of cancer?
Indeed I do, but not of body as you thought:
Far worse is wasting of the heart.

More or Less?

In front of you stands a woman,
deep, wise, brimming with love,
offering herself to you.

Why do you hesitate and look for less,
when you are starving
and she is food?

Pain

Yes it hurts
when you choose company with others, or yourself,
above mine,
when no dinner awaits my homecoming,
and no glad words are spoken,
when you warm to me
only the hour you think you'll get lucky.

Similarities and Differences

How much I have learned in your arms.
The blessing of the body you have practiced,
just this, the love of flesh
soft and warm and hidden places.

Even more I have learned apart
where only the gift of today awaits.

No Illusions

Gates snap shut in my heart.
I watch them detached,
as I discover you are human.

How freeing to finally have the bubble break.
No illusions!
Now we can get down to the nuts and bolts of love.

Valour

Courageous are the ones
who endure a pain-filled body uncomplaining,
who face death with grace and dignity.

Brave are those who live alone;
no parents, children, or partners loving them,
who rise each day praising God's gifts.

No less than these are lovers,
who keep their hearts open
to be broken again and again.

Stage Three: Non-Attachment

No longer do I think of you
hourly.
No longer do I need to call,
or for you to call me.

My eyes now roam
seeking another man,
and yet they don't.

When I was young
these signs would herald the end.
But now, without rules,
I wait open to the universe's plans.

Between Two Knowns

In love; out of love,
somewhere between the two I dwell,
receptive and detached,
in complete ignorance
of what is being worked
on me, on you, on us.

For once in my life
my preference is not knowing the answers,
nor anticipating an outcome,
but in savouring
the unfolding gift of Now.

Three Possibilities

If you are my last love and this love ends,
I am glad we had these days.

If there is another coming
and you, like John,
are preparing the way
I am grateful.

And if, in a future time, love blooms for us again
I, like a flower
will open after the long night.

The Truth

If I were truthful I'd hold you
and whisper that I am empty
in places we don't meet,
where no sweet words allowed
finally quelled my ardour.

If I were truthful I'd say
you've awakened in me a suppressed hunger
for merging, intimacy-love in all forms,
known only through commitment of many years,
or through grace.

What I'm trying to say is "Thank you".

Ups and Downs

Two months into dating,
nary an argument in sight,
while snuggling on the couch, you say,
"I don't think this will be a long-term relationship."

Given that you are an intuitive guy, honourable, honest,
wanting to cause me no pain,
I take notice and rein myself in–
no attachment to a future with you.

But my heart, listening with deeper wisdom,
will not obey.
It knows grief speaks; losing your last love,
and fearing loss again.

Four months into relationship,
still grieving, you try those words once more.
No longer shocked into silence, trusting the heart, I reply,
"I will only leave if you are unhappy with me."

"Never," you respond, moving to hold me,
"You are a blessing in my life."

Stage Four: Companionship

Tromping through forest
gathering mushrooms:
chanterelles, boletus, and the last oysters.
What a perfect day
getting dirty and tired together.

Pulling out food from my fridge and yours,
cooking who knows what,
drinking from chateau cardboard.
Who needs a first-class restaurant
when we have this?

Early morning chats drinking our coffee
filling our cups to the brim with love.
Nothing special–just planning the day
of grass cutting and writing emails
ten minutes, or so, of solid comfort.

Gratitude

Your toothbrush moved to my place this week,
my slippers to yours.
I've learned my way around your kitchen,
as you have in mine.

Scratching my feet, rubbing your hand,
all sorts of little affections,
that are dearer to me than a child's smile,
or the Taj Mahal.

Between the Sheets

Tenderly we flow together
blending our energies,
stroking and kissing all parts
of the other,
feeling their pleasure as our own.

Chatty Kathy

Afterwards…lying in bed,
you falling asleep,
Chatty Kathy emerges.
"Blah Blah Blah" and on it goes.

"Um" you reply
with the occasional "Uh Huh" thrown in.
Both satisfied, laughing at ourselves,
we close our eyes once more.

A Gentle Man

Arms loaded with zucchinis and tomatoes
you arrive at the door.
White Bwana returns from the hunt
grinning with pleasure to share his abundance.

Out with the frying pan and teriyaki
creating your first-ever recipe;
a great feed, enough for us and many more.

Then, gathering up dirty dishes,
graceful as a cat, you glide to the kitchen
and begin to wash up.

Each gesture and kindness
open my heart, till overflowing it whispers,
"I love this man."

In Love and Love

Being in love and love are different.

The first breaks all bounds,
soars and falls,
knows no peace,
ecstatic, hungry, playful,
like a nestling on its maiden flight
discovering the heights.

The second is like the calm ocean
humming to the heartbeat of the Earth,
deep and profound,
dependable and true,
neither peaks nor valleys
disturbing the day.

Embraced by Philia

Recovering from surgery,
grateful for this time watching tulips grow,
caressing the cat who drools blissfully,
noticing each passing car.

Experiencing old age at thirty-six–
what a gift!

We Never Loved Like This Before

Embracing without kissing,
separated by thirty years,
my first love calls,
filling me with wonder.

This compassionate man,
no longer closed,
tired from giving gifts to so many
seeks solace in my heart.

More right than right,
returning now with gamey knee,
and me, wrinkled and arthritic,
both ripened by life,
we touch once more.

Two Men

Absent by day, a healer by night, the green man
teaches non-attachment to a slow student.
Now, my first love appears,
soothing heart tears with sweet words.
Are two men really needed?
What a case I am!

One for the body and one for the soul,
One from the present and one from the past,
the pair, each precious,
greedy lady, really two?

One widowed, who was happy.
One married, happily.
Both here in my life, their choice.
But aren't two, one too many?

And...umm...is either right?
Of course they are.
Would the divine not know what is needed?
Silly woman, they're both for you.

Dream Lovers

Celibate in all ways,
I live alone by choice.
God, the Earth, all Beings
no preference have I by day.

Days, then weeks and months go by
with never a thought of men.
Happy, content, enjoying 'what is'
and then strange things begin.

When I sleep at end of day
my body seeks to eat,
to draw to it dream lovers
to feed when not awake.

I watch this dance, unmoved
to see what food today–
young, old, known or not
come and go for me.

Here a hug, there a touch
and sometimes fertilized
the juices flow, and yet I know
my body is not me.

Observing all, I feed the child
in this I have a stake.
'Tis only fair to love the one
that houses me awake.

Dark Thanksgiving

You are empty and feel the loss
of deep love.
Sunken, depressed and grieving,
you are cut adrift,
not knowing who you are.
Ah, what a wonderful time
for the universe to work its magic.

Dear friend, stay open,
eat forbidden fruit,
throw away old roles and be naughty.
Only remember to be grateful
and thank spirit daily for its many gifts.

As Mortality Hovers

I'm in a sour mood.
Fear of death knots my stomach.
You with cancer weigh on me.
Going there, staying here,
all the same.

Your dying kills me too.
A shared youth, brother-friend.
Old today,
no matter how many sea lions roar
and kingfishers dive.
Coffee and chocolate cannot dull the pain of ending.

Is there time to speak of you and me?
Or should I follow your lead and keep it light
as if a million days await?

Then the anger and tears begin:
that with all my skills,
I can find nothing to do or say
that means a thing.

Mammisi

Listening to a woman with Alzheimer's
I cried for you tonight.
She too yet remembers
as into the darkness she goes.

And you, Mom, dear friend
cherished in my heart,
I remember those last years:
fading memory, failing body,
past complaint, humour intact,
humility and quiet pride,
teaching me still;
dying before death.

*Mammisi is my pet name for my mother.
It means 'house of birth' in ancient Egyptian

To Mother

Did I take you for granted?
Did I neglect you?
Did I overlook your pain?
Did I berate your softness?
Did I chastise your weakness?

Did you know how much I love you?

Grieving Your Absence

Sharing a glass of wine,
sitting together for dinner,
chats on the sofa,
holding your hand:
these memories I treasure.

But best of all was your kiss goodnight.

Lucie

On Santa Lucia's day, sprawled on a heating pad in a shoebox,
the baby lovebird arrived.
"Could you look after her for the weekend?"
asked my exhausted friend, handing her over.

Falling out of the nest, abandoned by parents,
needing to be fed every four hours,
the little preemie was doomed to extinction.
No time for one when you raise hundreds.

Setting the alarm clock, I committed to motherhood,
all weekend carrying the naked nestling
under my sweater close to my heart.
By Monday I'd fallen in love.

As feathers sprouted, her outings began
up the bra strap and out the neck,
staring curiously at the new world
before descending again for comfort.

Longer forays to the shoulder,
loving nibbles on neck and ears,
fascinated by earrings, mine and everyone else's.
Lucie loved all visitors, claiming humans as hers.

Playing hide and seek behind dishes,
rolling marbles across the floor,
chewing ends off shoelaces,
happily entertaining herself...for a while.

I, working two floors up
hear her call, "Ca Ha, Ca Ha?"
This, translated into lovebird lingo, means,
"Where are you?"

I wait. A few minutes later,
having hopped up the stairs of Everest,
Lucie, the conquering hero, waddles through the doorway,
and ascends the pant leg onto my shoulder.

Sammy

Through the day my mind turns to Sam.
Does he wait for me to come?
Is he thinking of me, as I of him?
Will he be sad if I renege?

Finally, mid-afternoon, sun ebbing in the winter sky
I lace on hiking boots, grab pole and leave.
Tap, tap, does he hear me yet?
Inheld breath, I walk to his drive.

He looks up awaiting my invitation.
"Yes," I say in thought and word
and he, joy flooding his face,
lopes toward me wagging his tail.

To Wayshowers

As I travel the unknown path
I remember others who have gone before.
They wait ahead just beyond sight,
with open arms and hearts they hail me.

They salute all progress, they cry at all failures.
They befriend me, who travels alone.
Their deeds are guideposts on the way.
Their words leave echoes in the breeze.

These are a warrior breed, stout hearted and good,
patient in waiting, persistent in striving.
If I lag behind, they urge me forward.
When I fall, they lift me up.

Can I lose faith while they stay near?
Can I deceive when they see all?
I can only fail through lack of will.

Ode to Nutcrackers

Take or leave what a teacher says,
Choose to come or go.
There is no price to pay, no obligation.
Be free like a butterfly,
sampling the nectar of many flowers.
There is a time for this when young.

But then we grow,
serve our soul, serve the world.
Now we need a teacher to light our path.
A wise one, a fool, does it matter?
Commitment to love cracks open our heart,
not love's object.

Still... choose wisely for the best nutcracker.

A Good Teacher

He hits them. He cuddles them.
He yells and cries and laughs.
They ask to stay and he says, "Leave."
They wish to leave and he says, "Stay."

He says one thing and does another–
no ritual, nor meditation, nor teachings–
just sit and eat what he gives you.

Embraced by Agape

Let me be a rose
inviting you to visit,
a mirror
to see yourself clearly,
and a doorway into your soul.

Gold Filings

I am the magnet and you the gold filings
drawn to me.
You are the magnet and I the gold filings
drawn to you.
My soul, your soul—all
drawn to God.

Why speak of your lead, reminding me?
I see your gold transformed by alchemy.
You can never leave me and I'll never leave you
for God is the magnet and we the gold filings.

Comrades on the Path

Holding hands we journey
in fog and sunshine
up the mountain and down again.
The end no longer binds us.

Now we've got it. Now we don't.
Speeding up, slowing down,
laughing, crying, learning, growing–
how far we've come together.

How can I not love you
when God working through you
transforms me.

Dress Up

These clothes I wear are not me.
A child plays 'dress up' for the world:
lover, tyrant, mother, friend,
all come and go for me.
I put them on, take them off, no matter,
giving you what you need.

Dear ones, stay longer, dive deeper.
Inside your heart, when you find you
you'll find me too.

The Mirror

Told I was generous, I gave more.
Praised for ethics, my standards rose.
Lauded for patience, it too increased.
"Your laugh is contagious," they said.
I laughed all the more.

Obviously, I am what you see.

Hold Your Note

People see what they want.
Compromising, sacrificing,
bending over backwards,
make no difference.

Remain steadfast in your truth.
Hold your own note
and some, having loved you and left
will return again-or not.

Feast on Me

Eat me up
till there's nothing left.
First the juicy bits,
then the gristle.
Stuff yourself,
even the crumbs.

Rebirth

Do not second-guess spirit;
your lists of preferences
mean nothing.

Spirit is not interested in your comfort,
but in breaking you apart
until your shell crumbles
and you are reborn as love.

Awakening from Success

You envy my success
you who live in hardship.

Yes, everything I've ever wanted I have.
Nice home, good friends, work I enjoy,
recognition near and far,
money enough for me and many more.

Ah, you think it's easy
being shackled to the world.
To awaken from success, rather than pain,
in truth, is harder by far.

September Melancholy

Melancholy grabs.
Cursed with Celtic blood of drinkers and poets,
singers and depressives,
I'm occupied by moods of loss.

Emptiness stares me down.

Collapsing, I wonder
if throwing everything away and journeying
a penitent to India or Compostela
would cure me?

Choices

Distracted by happy and sad–
equally untrustworthy.
In a deep ocean
sinking.

Should I struggle to surface,
to gulp air,
or surrender to death once more,
letting go hope of life,
and retreat to dark Silence
where Nothing moves.

Enjoy the Day

I've toppled again.
Not even spiritual books
    ecstatic bliss
    dedicated work
    recognition by teachers
have rid me of this personality.

No effort of any kind
has helped me.
I might as well enjoy the day.

Loving the World

I can't imagine sitting in bliss,
missing the world.
There is time for that–between lives, another life–
Not now.

Do I doubt the wonder?
Not at all.
Do I disbelieve the Saints?
Of course not.
Then why delay?
Why cling to this world?

It's my work, my love, that's all:
being me in the world,
being I in spirit,
balancing the two.

A Prayer for God's Grace

Gifts given by God
can be neither demanded nor cajoled.
Why anticipate, you who know nothing of the plan?
Why practice unending ways to prove yourself worthy?

God needs no proof–
Minute by minute He knows your heart.
Your tricks won't work–So start!
Strip off deceits and bare your throat.

Salute to Death

"I'll accept less," I bargain with Death;
He does not look at me.
"Okay," say I, "I think I'll cry."
Unmoved he sits, for all to see.

"Damn you," I shout, "I'll not stay true
to those who won't help me."
Then I pause and listen hard
with hope that he'll agree.

A gaping hole confronts me now
He's got me by the neck.
He shakes, and shakes, and shakes back sense
until I hear the break.

Insight

Questing outside leaves you empty.
Questing inside does too.
Ergo, questing is pointless.

Stay still in one place.
See what happens, or doesn't.
Change nothing, hope for nothing.
Stop everything that keeps you clinging to life.

Then, and only if it be your destiny,
grace might enter.

Day of Liberation

Awake in sleep,
asleep when awake,
boundaries are breaking away.

A little more effort
in both of these states
would certainly hasten D-Day.

The Beloved

Almost midnight when
God speaks loudest in Silence.

Winking and retreating like a teasing lover
beckoning and seducing with promises of riches
never seen, not known...only hoped for.

Allow

Allow the day to pass, watching it
sunrise to sunset and into the dark,
being one with the Sun and Earth
in clockless time.

How many days do we live this in a life?
Children forget to be and learn to do,
returning in old age as senility and death beckon.

Unwilling, we are forced to our knees by time
relentlessly pushed to submit to 'what is.'

Much better to enjoy now while we still can choose to savour the depths and heights of a day–any day– Perfect.

Message for Doubting Thomas

There are Masters
who have lived for hundreds, even thousands of years,
Right here. Right now.

There are men and women
with remarkable powers of healing and sight,
Right here. Right now.

Poor Thomas, he thinks he knows better.

Cease Talking and Listen

Why speak when words are no longer true?
Round and round you circle
near, far, never reaching shore.

Talking will not work!
You can never know while you stay on the surface
maintaining a safe distance
from truth.

Dear heart, dive deeper into Silence
where no words, no thoughts, await.

Playing with Matter

No rules hold me.
I rise, fall, build and tear down.
I hold, release, yearn and hold again.

Gently, firmly, it's all the same.
Playing with matter, that's the game.

Rainbow Dust

Skirting your issues, circling your core
leads to endless illusion.
But, 'Who am I?' is an arrow
piercing the veil
killing you dead.

Fears of greater and lesser disappear
only 'What is' remains.
Nothing to defend, nor uphold,
only rainbow dust of God everywhere.

Do You Want This?

Beyond the door
Nothing.
    Nothing to speak
    Nothing to hear
    Nothing to touch nor taste.
Beyond the door
    Peace
    Stillness
    Silence
All that is wanted
and all that is not.

The Last Word

Journey beyond the journey.
Leap into Nothing!
Embrace the Void!
Your love, your mother, and you are found

and lost
and found again
dissolving and reforming forever.

Sitting on a park bench–
as good a place as any
to await the body's reconfiguration after death.

Quatrains

God severs every cord,
shatters all desires,
removes all temptations,
neuters me for Him.

1. How can I help you?
    suspicious
        conceited
            scared
                complacent–
There is no room to insert the arrow!

2.
Who can tell teenagers anything?
They will not listen
to truth, to love, to threats.
Nothing will move them from their path.

3.
Surrendering technique:
do's and don'ts–
watching them melt into the Void
and waiting to follow.

4.
Softening the fringes towards the centre,
heart awaiting its Beloved.
No teacher, nor teaching, can teach this.

5.
The fire burns away the dross of centuries.
Don't stop!
Burn hotter, faster,
until all is gone
leaving only God.

6.
Let me dream of far away:
fair lands I seek,
kind hearts to know,
no more pain, regret, constraint,
no more No's.

7.
Wild waves roll in
    crashing against the shore
    bashing boundaries
    that surround me.
How I long to be broken by God.

8.
It no longer matters what I do:
all deeds are the same—no good, no bad,
all actions complete in themselves,
and never complete.

9.
Judging your accomplishments through others' eyes
has not made you happy.
Why do you quote them?
Has it convinced you or me?

10.
It's a role to be 'the knower,'
just as certain as to be 'the friend.'
Give it away!
Stand naked!
Nothing crowning you.

11.
The rich man wants more:
What does he pay to gain the Light?
What is the cost to live in Truth?
All must he give, or go on his way.

12.
Move consciously
through blue-black space,
to find the universe within.

13.
I think not, therefore I AM
is the real truth.

14.
Flowing like the river
downstream we go
until at last we rest, past eddies and rocks
in the ocean's calm breast.

Embraced by Nature

I love this world:
soft colours of sunrise, still evenings,
tinkling brooks and roaring waterfalls.

Plunging my nose inside the hyacinth
I enter bliss.

Wake up!

A sunny day mid-February
calls me outside to the garden.
Snowdrops up early this year, crocus too.

The first robin returned days ago,
now flocks cover the grass seeking worms.
Paired birds sit gobbling food,
storing fat for nesting.

Dark pink buds grow on quince,
green shoots shove through dead plants.
Leaves and debris call to be raked,
wet soil to be turned.

In the air, grasping life,
another spring is born.

Amaryllis

For weeks I wait for signs of life.
Finally four leaves emerge, growing tall, then taller.
What, no blossom?

I think about throwing it out.
Only then, unwatched and unwatered
the bud begins to form.

Birth of the Day

Streaming from black-holed space
sunrise fills my face.
Glorious promise of hope,
unceasing new beginnings.

Chirping, cawing, buzzing start:
God opens the day.

Two Days at Best

Ladybugs are dying around me.
You lie on the carpet
reminding me: one, two days at best—
that's all you've got.

Ode to Rhubarb

In two weeks rhubarb goes from nothing
to dessert.
Unlike us, it knows its purpose.

Bravery or Trust

Tiny birds with stocky bodies and short tails
fly together in woods
fluttering here and there
searching for food on the forest floor.

They let me stand and watch them,
fearless or trusting
I'm not sure which.

One hops closer and pecks my boot.
Not finding it tasty, it flutters away
leaving me full.

Birds I Loved Today

I rescued a young finch trapped in the shed,
and carrying it outside
felt its beating heart.
Stunned, it sat on the grass,
then slowly, very slowly, glided away.

A spotted thrush crashed against the glass
and fell to the ground.
Gently, I held it
and with blood running down my hand,
witnessed its last breath.

So much beauty in one day.

Winter Feeding

Birds eat most just after dawn.
Kingfishers, waiting to strike,
hover like hummingbirds
above waves.

Jays bully each other at the feeder
screaming "mine, mine,"
while little sparrows wait their turn.

And off by himself, one lone robin,
having arrived too early,
stands confused in the snow.

Abundance

Bird book and binoculars in hand
I peer out my front window.
Sea birds in plenty sail by
but no little ones approach.

Patiently I wait,
eyeing the sprouting tulips daily inching higher.

Finally, tired of sitting, I open my back door.
There they are–robins, flickers and more,
happily eating the worms.

The Eagle Doesn't Give Up

First awake this morning–
almost dark–it takes to flight,
scanning the waters for life.

Claws extended, watching, waiting, it dives
and misses.
Climbing, it hovers, circles, and dives again
and misses.

Rising, it lands on a high branch,
watching, waiting,
as the dance of life and death continues.

Always Another Fish

Barking seals, waves lapping;
a crane stands in the shallows.

No rush, no greed, no fear:
always another fish awaits.

The Nervous Doe

Deer standing at edge of forest
beckoned by the sad man to stay.
Fearing her life she comes forward
step by step.

Say only sweet things:
call her precious,
gently open your heart
which she hears louder than words
summoning her.

When Civilization Meets Nature

Walking on the bluffs on a warm autumn day,
cresting the hill, I see you on the rocks,
silent and still.
"My Gawd," I panic inside, "I hope you're not injured."

Slowly, not to startle you, I inch closer.
You turn deep ocean eyes towards me
and pierce my depths,
while I calculate how to carry you to the vet.

Sicker and heavier you become with each step I take.
You, all the time, watching me.
Finally, ten feet from each other, you've had enough
and slide into the sea, effortlessly.

About the Author

Tanis Helliwell M.Ed. is the founder of the International Institute for Transformation (IIT), which offers programs to assist individuals to become conscious creators to work with the spiritual laws that govern our world. IIT programs are offered in Canada, the United States, Mexico, Germany, Britain, Italy, Holland, France and Ireland.

Tanis Helliwell is the author of *Summer with the Leprechauns: A True Story; Take Your Soul to Work; Decoding Destiny: Keys to Mankind's Spiritual Evolution*, and soon to be published *Pilgrimage with the Leprechauns: A True Story of an Irish Tour*. She is a student and teacher of the Inner Mysteries, living on the seacoast north of Vancouver, Canada. For over twenty years, she has led people on tours and walking pilgrimages to sacred sites.

Since childhood, she has seen and heard elementals, angels, and master teachers on other planes. For sixteen years she conducted a therapy practice, helping people with their own personal spiritual transformation.

In addition to her spiritual workshops, she is a sought-after keynote speaker and has worked for almost thirty years as a consultant to businesses, universities and government, both to create healthy organizations, and to help people develop their personal and professional potential. Her clients include IBM, McKinsey and Company, David Suzuki Foundation, Ministry of Fisheries and Oceans, University of Calgary, The Banff Centre- Leadership Programs.

Her work is committed to helping people to develop right relationships with themselves, others and the Earth.

Write to the author, order books, CDs and DVDs, or for information on tours and workshops, please contact:

Tanis Helliwell
C4 Hollingsworth Rd., RR #3 Powell River, BC., Canada
V8A 5C1
E-mail: tanis@tanishelliwell.com
Web site: www.tanishelliwell.com

BOOKS:
Summer with the Leprechauns: a true story CDN $20
Take Your Soul to Work CDN $20
Decoding Destiny CDN $20

CDs
Series A - Discovering Yourself: 2 visualizations
1. Path of Your Life / Your Favourite Place
2. Eliminating Negativity / Purpose of Your Life
3. Linking Up World Servers / Healing the Earth

Series B - The Inner Mysteries: Talk and visualization
1. Reawakening Ancestral Memory / Between the Worlds
2. Celtic Mysteries / Quest for the Holy Grail
3. Egyptian Mysteries / Initiation in the Pyramid of Giza
4. Greek Mysteries / Your Male and Female Archetypes
5. Christian Mysteries / Jesus Life: A Story of Initiation

Series C - Sacred Earth Talk and visualization.

Individual CDs - CDN $20
Series A (3 items) CDN $55
Series B (5 items) CDN $90

DVDs and VIDEO CASSETTES:
1. Take Your Soul to Work
2. Managing the Stress of Change
Individual DVDs and Videos CDN $20

plus postage and handling